Bank Street Gosler Hall
Tillicoultry

Prize Awarded to

Maurice Hunter

"Joy-Time" Competition

March 1961.

HORSEMAN OF THE KING

JOHN WESLEY COMES TO PREACH

HORSEMAN OF THE KING

The Story of John Wesley

by
CYRIL DAVEY

LUTTERWORTH PRESS
LONDON

First Published 1957
Second impression 1958
Third impression 1959

A film-strip on John Wesley can be had through COMMON GROUND, 44 Fulham Road, London, S.W.3; No. CGA347.

MADE AND PRINTED IN GREAT BRITAIN BY
EBENEZER BAYLIS AND SON, LIMITED, THE
TRINITY PRESS, WORCESTER, AND LONDON

FOR
SUSAN

CONTENTS

1

THE RESCUE

MILES away across the flat Lincolnshire countryside people in tiny, squalid cottages could see the flames rising into the air. Those who lived far away shrugged their shoulders and went back to sleep on the straw-filled sacks they used for mattresses. Someone's house in Epworth was on fire, that was all. It would be put out before they could reach it over the water-logged fens.

In Epworth the news passed from one house to another, and men and women rushed out to join in the excitement. Sparks flew into the air from the dry thatch. Smoke billowed up into the moonlit sky. As they got nearer to the house they could hear the cries of men mingling with the frightened crying of the animals.

"The Rectory is on fire!"

More than one man made the same answer. "A very good thing, too. Let it burn. Serve old parson Wesley right!"

Samuel Wesley, the Rector of Epworth, was not much liked by most of his people. He was too interested in books, for one thing, while they were only concerned with the hard work they had to do from light till darkness in the fields. He was

9

narrow-minded, too, they said, and they hated him for the way he attacked their cock-fighting and bull-baiting and their evil ways in his sermons. More than once the rough villagers had tried to drive him out of his parish. They had burgled the house, burned his corn-ricks and wounded his cows and horses in their spite against his quiet goodness. Now, on this winter night in the year 1709, they had set fire to the Rectory itself.

Fortunately, there were still friendly folk who were willing to help at such a time. The animals were dragged to safety from the blazing stables and barn. Neighbours with buckets of water rushed to the house from the pond nearby to try and quench the flames, though there was no hope of their putting them out. Mrs. Wesley stood with her children round her—Molly, Hetty, Nancy, Patty, Emilia, Sukey and little Charles. Their faces were white and frightened, in spite of the glow from the flames, and they stared, without moving, towards the door of the house. Samuel Wesley himself was nowhere to be seen.

Suddenly, silence fell on everyone. The Rector staggered out from the house, his dark clothes singed by the fire, and his arm across his eyes.

"I can't get to him," he cried. "The stairs are burning." Then, he dropped to his knees and began to pray.

The fire had been discovered in the middle of the night. Samuel Wesley and his wife Susannah had managed to waken the children and hustle them outside. They roused the servants and set them to work to save anything they could drag out of the house. It was only when they looked round that they discovered that little John—Jackie as they called him—was missing. He had been sleeping by himself in a back room at the top of the house. His father had dashed back to try and get him out, but it was too late. No one could save him now. The whole house would be alight in a moment. The other children fell on their knees, like their father, asking God to help.

"Look!" The cry came from Mrs. Wesley. "Up there at the window! It's Jackie!"

A little boy, not yet six years old, stood quietly looking down at the crowd from an upstairs window. He had been wakened by the noise, and run to the front of the house. Too tiny to jump, he waited for help. A man rushed forward, scrambled on to a second man's shoulders, and leaned up to the window. Five-year-old Jackie jumped into his upstretched arms. He was saved.

Almost before his father had got up from his knees, and Mrs. Wesley had thrown her arms round the little boy, there was a tremendous crash. The roof had fallen in. Jackie had made his escape with hardly a second to spare.

Mrs. Wesley—and, indeed, all the family—felt that there was some great purpose of God in such a wonderful deliverance from death. Jackie never forgot that night. He described himself as "a brand plucked from the burning". He believed God had saved him because He had something for him to do. Before he died, more than eighty years later, the whole of England knew that he was right.

* * *

The fire was by far the most exciting thing that happened while John Wesley was growing up in Epworth. He belonged to a quiet family in a part of England which few people knew anything about, far from London, where his older brother Samuel was at school, and away from the busy towns. Apart from cock-fights, fairs and savage boxing matches, to which the Wesley children never wanted to go, life passed smoothly in Epworth year after year. The family crest, with its cross and scallop shells, proved that there were ancestors who had centuries before been pilgrims to the Holy Land, but now the Rector's family, descended through their father and mother from some of England's noble families, were so poor that there was hardly enough money to buy food and clothes for them all. Fourteen children had been born before John, and four more were born afterwards. Rector Wesley tried to earn some extra money by writing books and poems, but few people bought what he wrote and, more often than not, he was in debt.

Now and again the Rector made long journeys to London, riding the narrow muddy roads on his old horse, in the hope of persuading booksellers to publish some of his verses. His long, disappointed face told the family, as soon as they saw him ride back into the yard, that he had had no success. Once, he was away from home for a worse reason. He was put in prison in Lincoln because he could not pay his bills, and Mrs. Wesley and the children had to go and visit him in the dark, crowded, smelly gaol. They found him preaching to the other prisoners. Little John was horrified at what he saw.

"One day," he said to his mother, "I'm going to preach like Father. And I'm going to do something for poor people who are in prison, too." It would be a long time before the chance came, but he was to keep his word.

* * *

With a husband so often away from home, and who preferred writing in his study to doing anything else when he was in the house, it was Mrs. Wesley who really counted in the children's lives. She was mother, friend and school-teacher to them all. She kept them very much in order, too.

In the kitchen were two tables, a small, low one, set with spoons and plates, and the bigger one with knives, forks, plates and pewter mugs. The smaller children sat at the little table, but even there they had to keep the rules. There was silence while they ate, unless the Rector or Mrs. Wesley spoke. Children were seen, but not heard. Every now and again there was meat, though not every day. At the little table one of the girls rattled her spoon on her plate, louder than she need have done. John looked at her in surprise. Her plate was empty, and she moved her spoon noisily again. The serving-maid came towards her.

"No!" Mrs. Wesley's voice was sharp, and the maid backed away, the meat-dish still in her hands.

The children were allowed more if there was more to spare—and if they were asked by the serving-maid. They were never allowed to call to her, nor to ask. Rattling the spoon counted as "asking". The little girl would hear more of it in her "half-hour".

Mrs. Wesley's "half-hours" were part of the family's life. John's was on Thursday evening. Every week, on that day, little John would go to his mother's room, exactly on time, not a minute early or late, and knock on the door. He would enter when she called, bow politely to her, and sit on the stool in front of her. Exactly half an hour later he would leave. In the time he spent with her, his mother would talk about the week that had passed since he was last with her. There were sharp words about his failures and a little praise for what had been good. But John, too, could talk frankly about his problems and his dreams. They discussed the book he was reading, the part of the Bible he had been studying, and what could be done to help some person in need. John always felt better for the Thursday half-hour, and years later he wrote to his mother wishing he could turn to her in the same way at the same time to discuss bigger problems than he ever thought he would have to face.

It may sound like a very severe household. Certainly it was orderly. More than that, it was happy. The children played in the barn, the farmyard and the dovecote. Mrs. Wesley was lovely to look at, and they thought her the most wonderful person in England. They learned to think carefully, to behave politely, to do things for others and to serve and fear God. Very few households in the country were as charming and happy, and few, perhaps, were as clever. What they were, they owed very largely to their mother.

*   *   *

One winter's day in January, 1714, little John, just over ten years old, had to leave this friendly house and set out on the beginning of his great adventures. He was going to school—a proper and famous school, this time, not one where he would sit with girls and outshine them all. His mother had taught them all, beginning on their fifth birthday, in the Rectory kitchen. Now he was going to prove himself in a bigger world.

His father was already on the horse when John, warmly wrapped against the snow, came out of the house. John was heaved on to the back of the big horse, clutched his father's back, waved to his mother and sisters and then, clip-clopping out of the yard, they were on their way to London. It was four days later when John, almost too stiff to get down from the horse, after riding along the snow-bound, frosty, rutted roads, alighted before the double gates of Charterhouse, where he was to spend the next six years of his life. Not until he became a "gown-boy" in the famous school did John realize how happy he had been at Epworth.

In his black cloth, baize-lined gown and dark knee-breeches he sat solemnly in his seat in the chapel or worked at his desk. There were forty-four other "gown-boys" in his house, and none of them had learned politeness in a rectory school-room. They thought him very prim and proper, but he was probably no worse treated than any other small boy in the school. All juniors were bullied by the big boys, as a matter of course. No one ever interfered with it. All small boys had their meat stolen by big boys. The smallest of all even had their bread taken by other juniors older than themselves. John hardly ever spoke of it in his carefully written letters home. It happened to everyone and was hardly worth mentioning.

Every morning of those six years, in sunshine or rain, a slim figure could be seen running round the Green in the school grounds, his auburn hair flying behind him. Three times he ran round it each day —exactly a mile. He had promised his father to do it in order to keep himself fit and, to the end of his life, John never broke his promises. Besides that, he thought it did him good, even though it gave him an appetite for more food than he was likely to have. No one else thought of doing it, but John never minded being different from other people if he thought he was right. It was the one thing that distinguished him from the other boys. He was never bottom in his lessons, and not often top. He had few close friends and had not really planned what he wanted to do when school was finished.

On the day he left Charterhouse, intending to go up to the university at Oxford, he said a quiet farewell to his masters and his school-fellows.

"We'll see you again sometime, I expect," they said.

No one would have imagined then that his name would be known to every man in England before the century was over and that it would be impossible to write the story of England in his time without referring to what he did.

2

CITY OF SPIRES

"LOOK!" cried John. "Isn't it beautiful?"

His companion, sitting by his side on the roof of the coach, looked at his eager face. John was only seventeen, setting out on the greatest adventure of his life so far. From the top of the coach they could see the spires of the churches and colleges rising into the air, graceful enough for a dream city.

"Yes, I suppose it is, the first time you see it. It's not so good when you reach it, believe me. What are you going to do at the university?"

John looked surprised at the stranger's question. "Why, sir, I shall study, of course. I hope to become a Master of Arts."

The man by his side laughed. "You'll be a very queer sort of student if you give your time to study, my lad," he said, sarcastically. "The only university men I've known spend their time at very different things—students and tutors, too!" He looked at John's clear-cut, intellectual face more closely. "But I believe you mean it, I really do. And what are you going to do when you've finished your studies, young fellow?"

John was hardly listening. His eyes were on the

town, drawing quickly nearer. "When I've finished? I don't know, sir. Perhaps I shall be a schoolmaster. At the moment I'm too excited to think. Look, sir, we're here in Oxford."

*   *   *

John very quickly realized why Oxford was regarded as one of the worst university towns in Europe. Its streets were narrow and dirty, the walls had posters advertising plays, balls and public hangings, and the lanes were thronged with girls shouting the familiar cries—"Buy a rabbit! A rabbit!" "Tender cucumbers, ripe for pickling!" "Buy my four ropes of hard onions!" John would have found the same kind of thing in any of the old cities of England. It was when he began to mix with the students that he found the stranger on the roof of the coach had been right. Most of the men in the university had far more money than he had, and they spent it all on pleasure. They dressed fashionably, drank hard and gambled heavily, sometimes right through the night. What shocked him most was that they drank and gambled and danced with the tutors who were supposed to be teaching them. As a result, examinations were a farce, and the surest way to pass at the end of their time at the university, so all students said, was to take the examining tutor out to dinner the night before, and give him a bottle of wine.

John was horrified. When he made it plain that he was going to work hard, most of his fellow-students laughed at him and, finally, left him alone. He had very little money for pleasure, and continued to dress in his plain clothes, to the amusement of the careless young men in their silks and satins. He was serious, honest and careful, and a regular attender at church.

It was when he was twenty-one that he wrote a letter to his parents which greatly surprised them. They had often wondered what he intended to do when he had finished at the university, but he never gave them any idea of what was in his mind. The Rector read the letter two or three times before he passed it over to his wife.

"Our John seems to have chosen his future at last," he said, quietly. "He says he wishes to become a clergyman of the Church of England."

"Like you!" Susannah Wesley took the letter and read it swiftly. "I hope he's right," she said. "He's very young to be ordained—only twenty-one."

"He's a good boy," put in the Rector. "He's honest and thoughtful. He works hard. And he loves God."

Susannah Wesley sighed. "Yes, Samuel, that is all true. But I wonder what he has to *give*, yet?"

John thought of the new life opening before him, and talked to his friends about it. One of them asked where he would like to have a church—in the town or the country?

"I hadn't really thought very much about that side of it," answered John. "If I have to look after a parish anywhere at all, I would like to have a quiet one somewhere in the country, where I can think and read, and perhaps do some writing." He looked out of the window at the college green beyond. "But what I'd really like would be to become a tutor here in Oxford, and spend the rest of my life here studying and teaching." He was more serious than ever, reading his Bible and saying his prayers regularly, hardly even taking time off to walk or ride in the lovely Cotswold country with his friends.

*   *   *

It was about this time that Charles, four years younger than his brother, came up to Oxford from Westminster School, in London. He and John were fond of each other, for all the rest of the family, apart from one brother very much older, were sisters. Charles bounced into his brother's room almost as soon as he arrived. He picked up the papers on John's desk, rushed across the room to look at his books, bounded to the window to look out.

"It's no use being angry with me for interrupting you, John," he cried. "I'm so excited, I can't stand still! Oxford, at last!" Then, looking at his brother, his handsome face grew serious. "John! You *do* look solemn! What's the matter with you?"

"Go carefully, Charles," John replied. "There are many temptations here for popular young men like you." He straightened the papers on his desk. "And please don't upset my papers every time you come into my room."

Charles laughed. "What an old stick-in-the-mud you've turned into, John. If that's what happens when you become a parson I hope I never turn into one. You look as if you've forgotten how to enjoy yourself." He put his arm through John's and led him towards the door. "Come and show me the sights of the town." John moved to the door with him, but his face was still serious. "What's the matter? Have you lost something?"

"No, Charles." John stood still for a moment. "I'm looking for something that I can't find!"

That was quite true, as Charles found out. John had hoped that by becoming a minister he would be happy and contented. Instead, he was depressed and worried. Preaching about God ought to have brought him joy; instead, it was hard work and he wondered if he ever helped anyone with what he said. It was as if God were a long way off, instead of being near at hand. Charles told him that it was perhaps because a university was not the best place to learn his new job. Surely the right spot for a minister was in a parish, with a church of his own, rather than in a study? When the Rector, now an old man, wrote to John and asked for his help in his Epworth parish John quickly agreed to go, hoping that he might find happiness dealing with the Lincolnshire country folk.

He soon found he was wrong. He disliked almost every moment of the two years he spent at Wroote, near Epworth. The people were ignorant and dirty, and cared nothing for the Church. The parsonage was damp, lonely and noisy with pigs, hens and sheep which huddled under his windows. It was a relief when he made up his mind to leave it all and go back to his work as a tutor at Oxford. At the university, he found that strange things had been happening, and that Charles was responsible for them.

*   *   *

Charles asked John to come round to his rooms soon after he arrived back in Oxford. "I want you to meet my friends," he said. Charles was still gay and handsome, but John found that he was very much more serious than he had been a couple of years previously. He crossed the green and knocked on Charles's door. It was opened almost at once. Inside, a dozen young men all jumped to their feet. John saw at once that they had been sitting round the table and that on it was an open Bible. They had been meeting regularly, they told him, to study the Bible together.

"The rest of the men in the university think we're quite mad, I'm afraid," Charles told him, "because we take our religion seriously."

"They've given us a nickname," put in another man. "They call us 'The Holy Club'."

A good-looking youth smiled, and John liked him at once. "That isn't the only name they call us," he said. "Because we try to live orderly lives, and go to church regularly, and not waste our time, they call us 'Methodists'."

"You *will* join us, won't you, John?" Charles's voice was urgent. "We need someone like you to help us—and perhaps we can help you, too."

Very quickly John became the leader of this group of earnest young students. He saw at once that they ought to do more than study the Bible and pray, and told them so. "Have you ever noticed the ragged children, as you pass through the streets?" he asked.

"You can't help seeing them. The town is full of them."

"I can manage to put down a little money each week," John went on. "If some of you do the same, we ought to be able to rent a room and start a school for them."

"But ragged children won't come to school—they'd be too ashamed of not having proper clothes," objected Charles.

"That's one of the reasons we need money," answered John. "We must try and buy—or beg—some clothes for them."

The school was begun, and the students and tutors began to have a new respect for the "Methodists". They were even more astonished at what they saw one early morning. For several days the town had been buzzing with the news of a public hanging that was to take place. Crowds lined the streets to watch the cart rumble by, with the condemned man in it, and hundreds of people were gathered outside where the hanging was to take place in full view of everyone. Slowly, as the cart rolled forward, the jeering grew silent. In the cart the people saw not only the murderer but two young men standing by his side, one of them very clearly a student and the other a tutor.

"Who are they?" The question was asked again and again.

One person knew the answer and it spread along the street. "It's John Wesley, from Lincoln College, and his brother. They've been visiting the prisons for months—preaching to the debtors and the thieves, and taking them food as well." The cart rolled by, taking the murderer to be hanged and the Wesley brothers to stand by his side. It was part of the work they felt they had to do; unpleasant as it was, it was just as much God's work as praying or preaching.

John was the leader in every part of the Holy Club's activities. Yet—he had to admit it to himself—he was still not happy. All his good works, and the friendship of the young men who looked up to him, had not solved his problems. God still seemed as far away as ever. He was being as good as he knew how to be—and yet there was something missing. It was just at this point that everything seemed to go wrong at once.

A letter from Epworth told them that the old Rector was dying. With his family round him, he died where he had spent most of his life. Susannah Wesley went to live with one of her daughters,

Emilia, not far away at Gainsborough. John refused to take over his father's parish, though he had no clear idea of what he wanted to do. Charles left Oxford, and when John returned to the university he found most of the Holy Club had left, too.

It was just then that he was introduced to General Oglethorpe.

3

JOHN FINDS THE SECRET

OUTSIDE the gates of St. James's Palace one
Sunday morning in 1735 there was the usual
group of sightseers—servants from the houses of
the great merchants who lived in the City of
London, or villagers from the farms and orchards
of Chelsea or Kensington. They hoped for a sight
of King George II or his queen, Caroline, and had
the excitement of recognizing the great people of
the day who drove, or were carried in sedan-chairs,
into the courtyard.

All at once, the country-girls giggled and the
townsfolk nudged each other. Amidst the men in
their bright coats and knee-breeches, and the ladies
in their huge hooped skirts, they saw a short,
solemn-faced man dressed soberly in black. He
wore a black three-cornered hat and no wig, and
under his arm he carried a huge book.

"Cheerful-looking fellow to come to the palace,
I *don't* think!" a girl said to the man who stood
with her at the gate.

The serving-man laughed. "Got a present for
the Queen under his arm, too!"

It was quite true. John Wesley was going to see
the Queen, and the volume he carried was the

book his father had been writing for years. John thought it was the greatest thing his father had ever written. He and Charles had waited in London for several weeks, staying with James Hutton, a friend who kept a bookshop, hoping for an appointment with the Queen. Samuel Wesley had dedicated his book to her and John wished to present it himself. In his heart he believed that she would be interested enough to do something for his mother, now that she was a widow and still very much in need of money.

Very nervously he entered the great room where, at the far end, Queen Caroline sat talking with her maids-of-honour. The colours of their lovely dresses in the sunlight were dazzling. John moved slowly and awkwardly across the room, knelt down and presented the big volume. He waited for her questions about his father and mother, and about the book itself. For a moment there was silence. He looked up. The Queen was looking at the cover.

"What a pretty binding you've chosen!" she said. Without opening it, she laid the book down. A moment later she was chattering to her ladies-in-waiting again. She did not even see John get up, bow, and back out of the room.

Back in the bookshop, John described what had happened. James Hutton and Charles listened with gloomy faces.

"So the Queen isn't going to do anything to help Mother after all!" said Charles.

John looked very grim. "I wonder how the Red Indians felt when *they* went to the palace," he muttered.

It was not very long since a group of Indians had been brought by General Oglethorpe from America—still, at that time, a British colony—to visit their King and Queen.

"Ah, yes, John!" Charles could not help laughing. "But they weren't dressed in parson's black!"

Even John smiled at that. The Indians had appeared in bright robes, scarlet and blue, with rabbit-fur edging and gold lacing. They had even insisted on appearing at the palace with their faces covered in war-paint. A moment later John was serious again.

"I keep on thinking of those Indians, you know, Charles," he said, slowly. "If only I could go to America and preach to them it would be something really worth doing. They know nothing of God, as we know Him."

"Why don't you, then?" James asked. "They need missionaries in America, surely?" He leaned forward. "You've made no plans for the future. You have no church to look after." He tapped John's knee. "Perhaps this is God's plan for you. Try and see General Oglethorpe!"

"Oglethorpe!" John sounded very thoughtful.

"He bought seven copies of Father's book on *Job*," put in Charles. "And he often helped

Father when he was short of money. Yes, John—
do write to him!"

*   *   *

Surprisingly enough, General Oglethorpe was
thinking of John Wesley at the same time, and it
was he, not John, who arranged that they should
meet. London's prisons were full of men who had
run into debt and could not pay their bills. Most
of them had no hope of ever getting out of prison
again. It was partly with such people in mind that
Oglethorpe persuaded the British Government to
set up a special colony in America called Georgia.
He had worked hard to clean up the Fleet, the
Marshalsea and the King's Bench Prisons in
London, but he knew that, even if the debtors were
set free, there was no work for them in England.
Overseas, in America, if Parliament would agree
to their being sent there, they would have a new
start and a new life. Eventually Parliament agreed
to the scheme, as long as other settlers were
allowed to go, too, and room was found for some
German refugees, called Moravians, who were
refugees from their own country. As soon as the
scheme was really launched General Oglethorpe
began to think of the men he would need to make
it succeed. He would need clergymen, certainly.
His mind turned to John Wesley, who had been so
interested in the debtors and prisoners at Oxford,
and had done so much for them.

At their first meeting, the soldier-governor

looked at the serious young clergyman. He felt that here was a sincere, religious man who could do a great deal for the new colony.

"Mr. Wesley," he said, quietly. "I want you to come to Georgia as a chaplain to the colonists. Will you come with us? We sail in October, in a ship full of debtors, Germans and families looking for a new life. You may be the very man we need!"

John sat upright. The general, like himself, was a man who wasted few words and came to the point quickly. "What about Charles, my brother?"

"I think I might be able to take him as my secretary."

To John, it seemed as if the world had changed. He could work as a missionary amongst the Indians as well as the settlers and, in America, he might very probably find the happiness he had never found in his work in England. Almost at once, he agreed that he would go. With Charles and two other ministers, who had been members of the Holy Club in Oxford, they sailed from Gravesend in October, 1735, on the beginning of their great adventure.

*   *   *

Less than eighteen months later a sailing ship dropped anchor off Deal, on the Kentish coast. A few passengers came ashore in a rowing boat and their baggage followed in another. One of the passengers was a slight, sad-looking man, in the dark clothes of a Church of England clergyman.

His face was thin and his eyes sunken, as though he had not slept well for a long time. In the inn, where he was to spend the night before riding on to London, he went straight away to his room.

John Wesley had come back to England. His adventure in America had gone wrong from the beginning. He had been a complete failure, and so had his brother. He was so miserable that he simply did not know what to do next.

There had been no opportunity to preach to the Indians. He found they were thinking of making war on the white men, and did not want to hear anything he had to say. Most of his time had to be spent trying to deal with the colonists, and John, just then, was the last person to help them. Mostly, they were rough men who had no interest in the Church and they disliked John Wesley and what they called his "narrow-minded ways". He had fallen in love, but the girl he would have liked to marry had married someone else instead. It would not have been so bad if Charles had been with him but, after less than a year, Charles felt he could not stand America any longer and had packed his bags and gone back to England. John was left alone.

Worst of all, he had not found the happiness he thought he would find. God did not seem to be any more real in America than He was in England. John made long lists of things he should do and not do. Sometimes he kept his "rules" and sometimes he did not, but it never made any difference. He

prayed and preached; he read his Bible and fasted.
He did all the things he thought would please God,
and yet he was unhappy because he felt he was
missing something. The German Moravians who
had sailed with them on the *Simmonds* all seemed
to have the secret he could not find, and that made
him more puzzled still. In a dreadful storm on the
way across the Atlantic, they had remained quite
calm when everyone, including himself, was
frightened that they were going to sink. In their
settlement in America they were just as peaceful
and happy. It seemed as though God was a per-
sonal friend of each one of them. John simply
could not understand it. He made up his mind to
look for some of the Moravians who had settled in
England when he eventually reached London, and
see if they could help him.

James Hutton, the Wesleys' bookseller friend,
introduced John to some of them, and took him to
some of the little Moravian meetings, where they
studied the Bible and prayed together. Slowly,
John began to get nearer to the end of his search
as he talked with them.

"You can't find happiness by trying to keep
rules," said one man. "You should be happy
because God loves you—and then you do the right
things because you love Him, too."

"You can't *earn* God's forgiveness by the things
you do—you must just accept His forgiveness if
you've done wrong," said another.

*   *   *

It was one Wednesday morning that John rose early, as he always did, and opened his Bible after he had dressed. He looked carefully at the words. They seemed to promise him that something wonderful was going to happen soon.

Just before he left home at breakfast time he picked it up again and let it fall open in his hand. He read what Jesus once said to a man who came to Him. "Thou art not far from the Kingdom of God." If only that were really true, he thought to himself, as he went out into the busy street.

That afternoon he climbed up the broad steps of St. Paul's Cathedral and pushed open the door. Inside, it was dim and quiet. He made his way to the front. The afternoon service was just beginning and the music echoed away up in the huge dome above his head. He listened carefully to the anthem. "Trust in the Lord . . ." He hardly heard the rest of the service. That was what other people had said to him. The way to know God was just to *trust* Him. When he came out of the dark building the May sunlight outside was bright on his eyes, and the street was crowded with people arguing and laughing at the stalls by the cathedral steps. He thought how good it would be to go for a long, lonely walk in the country just beyond Westminster, and think as he walked, but he had promised a friend to go to a meeting that night and it would never do to break his promise.

The sky was still coloured with the sunset as he set off from his lodgings for the little room in

Nettleton Court, just off Aldersgate Street, where the meeting was held. It was the last place he wanted to go, just then, for he had often been before to such meetings and gained little help. William Holland, one of the leaders, was standing up when he arrived, with a book on the table in front of him. He was going to read the introduction which Martin Luther had written centuries before to St. Paul's letter to the Romans. John sat down on one of the hard benches, wishing he had not come after all. Then, suddenly, he found himself listening carefully. A sentence or two seemed to stand out from all the rest. All at once, something happened, though he could never quite explain how or what it was. He sat up straight, and his eyes were bright. His face seemed to be filled with happiness. The people on each side of him looked at him and William Holland stopped reading.

"What is it, brother Wesley?" he asked.

"It was while you were reading," John answered, in a puzzled tone. "A wonderful feeling of peace and happiness came to me. I felt I *did* trust in Christ. My heart seemed strangely warmed!" He stood up, and looked round at them. "I have found it at last. I worked and preached, I visited the prisoners and went to America, to try and please God. And now, here in Aldersgate Street, in this little meeting, God is more real to me than He has ever been before." He moved towards the door. "Please forgive me if

I go. I must go and tell my brother what has happened." The door closed behind him, and the room was very quiet for a minute or two. John Wesley had found the secret. There seemed nothing they could say.

Charles Wesley was lodging just round the corner, in a narrow street named Little Britain. John, usually so dignified, ran along Aldersgate Street and down Little Britain as fast as he had ever done as a schoolboy at Charterhouse. As he reached the door of Charles's lodging he heard the clocks in the city begin to strike.

It was nine o'clock on the evening of the 24th of May, 1738.

4

NO PULPIT FOR JOHN

THE tall Prussian soldiers, made even taller by their high, pointed hats, sprang swiftly to attention as a sharp command came from the guard-room beside the town gate. Behind them were the walls of Halle, and an ancient gateway leading into the old town. Two men, very soberly dressed, came towards them, obviously wanting to enter the town.

"They are English," whispered one guard to the other, speaking in German. As the visitors approached there was another shout from the gateway and the guards moved into the road, barring the way with their bayonets. An officer stepped between them, speaking swiftly to the newcomers. The smaller of them replied in German.

"Names?"

"I am John Wesley. This is my friend Benjamin Ingham."

"Show me your passports." He held out his hand for the documents they produced. John and his companion were getting used to showing them to guards and soldiers. They had had to do it again and again, ever since they arrived in Germany.

"Where are you going? What are you doing? Why are you here?" The questions snapped, one after the other, from the tall officer.

"We have been invited to visit the Moravian settlements here in Halle, and at Marienborn and Herrnhut. I am to meet Count Zinzendorf, who you know is the leader of their Church, and to see something of their schools and their work for orphaned children."

"So!" The officer's voice softened. "They are good people, doing good work. You may go into the town. We have to be watchful for spies, you know." He handed their passports back. "I will send a soldier with you to show you the quickest way. This is an old town and you may easily get lost—though you speak very good German, *mein Herr*."

John might have answered that he spoke Spanish, too, and could read Italian and Portuguese, as well as Latin, Greek and Hebrew. He was never a man who showed off his cleverness, however, and with a word of thanks he followed the soldier into the narrow streets of the mediaeval city to meet the Moravians, of whom he had heard so much from his German friends in London and America. The results of his visit were to be very important in the years to come.

*   *   *

Back in England, he described to Charles some of the things he had seen on his three months' tour.

38

"They were just like the Germans we met on the boat going to America . . . just like those we found in America, too. They have the same joy in their hearts that you and I have found."

"What were these band-meetings you wrote about?" asked Charles.

"Ah! That's one of their most important ideas, I think. They all meet together in little groups, which they call 'bands'. Each group has a leader. Every week, when they meet, the leader asks them what they have done during the week, how God has helped them, what temptations they have conquered. As they talk together they help each other." John began to pace the room excitedly. "But they don't spend all their time talking, Charles!"

"You mean their schools and so on?"

"Our schools are not bad in England, but theirs are wonderful. If I ever began a school myself I would use some of their ideas. And they have orphanages, too. Wonderful places, where homeless children are looked after. We could do with something like that in England."

Charles sighed. "You may have to be a school-master yet, John," he said. "You have no church of your own, and you can't just spend your life going on tours to Germany, or preaching in other people's churches. Of course, you could go back to Oxford, if you wished." He got up and put his hand on John's shoulder. "What do you think God really wants us to do?"

"I don't know. But he will show us, Charles—I'm sure about that. Meanwhile, we must go on preaching." He looked at the pile of papers and the quill pen on the table, where his brother had been sitting. "And you must go on writing your hymns."

"Go on writing!" Charles laughed. "I can't stop writing, John! Hymns and poems just seem to pour off the end of my pen. I find myself making verses while I dress or wash or walk round the town." Suddenly he looked very serious. "But I can't think what good they are. Nobody ever sings them."

"God will have some use for your hymns, too, brother, when the time comes. As you say, we must just go on—writing and preaching."

*   *   *

That was not so easy as it sounded. Already many of the London churches no longer asked John to take their services. Instead of reading a quiet service, and a sermon from a book, during which the congregation could almost go to sleep, this new preacher seemed to be on fire and his sermons were too practical and forceful. They stabbed into the conscience of those who listened, and that was something they did not like. It seemed to be the same wherever he went.

Just after returning from Germany, John set out to take a morning service.

"I shall divide my sermon into two parts," he

told Charles, "preaching half this morning and half this evening."

The church was full, for the name of John Wesley was becoming well known in London. The buzz of conversation ceased as he went into the pulpit. There were no hymns, only some dreary chants, and few people sang. John wished he could teach them one of his brother's new hymns, with its gay, catching tune, but that, he knew, would raise almost a riot. The Church of England did not like hymns in its worship. Even so, what he told them in his sermon disturbed them almost as much as a hymn would have done. He looked at the well-dressed congregation, and told them they were sinful men and women, and that whatever they did or gave they could not please God unless they loved Him with their whole hearts.

Everywhere you could hear the same exclamation. "Sinners, indeed!" Wealthy, respectable people objected to a word they thought should only be used for thieves and vagabonds. Here and there, a man got up and stalked noisily out of the church. A group of ladies in their wigs and wide skirts followed them to the door, and stood chattering shrilly just inside. John went calmly on, talking of God's love and of his own new experience. He ended the service and came down the pulpit steps. As he did so, a man with a gold-topped staff stepped forward. He should have led the preacher out. Instead, he turned to the congregation.

"Do you want any more of this kind of preaching?" he asked, loudly.

From all over the church there were angry shouts.

"Then you shall not preach here to-night, as you planned to do, or at any other time, Mr. Wesley," the beadle said coldly. "I will see you out, and make sure that you do not come back!"

When John returned to his lodgings, Charles could see what had happened as soon as he looked at his brother's serious face. "Another church closed against us, eh, John?"

John sat down wearily, and nodded. "I must give them all I have to say at once in future, Charles," he said, with a wry smile. "They never give me a chance to put it into two sermons these days!"

"But we have so much to give the people, if they would only listen. We can offer them a new life. And they just don't seem to want it."

"It happens to everyone who wants to show people a new way of living, I suppose." John rose and looked out through the tiny panes of the window, with their bubbled glass, into the street below with its busy crowds. "But they do need God so much, Charles. Look at them! If only we could go out and tell *them* about Him. Most of them don't come into the churches, anyway."

"Listen to me, brother." Charles's voice was harsher than usual. "The church is the place for preaching God's word. If people won't come inside, they don't deserve to hear it. If you go on like that, you'll become like young George White-field." His handsome face was troubled. "And you know what people think of *him*!"

George Whitefield had been a friend of the Wesleys in their Oxford days and was now one of the best-known preachers in England. He had been to America, too, where they greatly liked him. Like Wesley, he had been forbidden to preach in the churches, but he simply could not be silent and now, in Bristol, he had begun preaching in the open air. In the fields and mining villages near the city, thousands of miners and country folk crowded to hear him.

"Oh, no, Charles!" John shook his head angrily. "That is one thing I could never do. Preaching in the open air is no way to worship God. I shall never do *that*!"

When a letter came from Bristol, shortly after-wards, John had a strange feeling that the simplest thing to do would be to leave it where it was, un-opened, on the table. It was important—something seemed to tell him that at once—but some-how he did not want to read it. When he did break the seal and open the thick sheet of paper he read it through two or three times before he put it down.

"It is from George," he said quietly. "George Whitefield."

"Is he in trouble?" asked Charles.

"Have they put him in prison for disturbing the

peace of Bristol?" asked James Hutton. "I always knew it would happen sooner or later."

"No, Charles. He is going to America again."

Charles rose from his chair, a smile on his face. "Then that's the end of field-preaching, John," he said cheerfully.

"It may not be, brother," replied John. "He has written to ask me to go to Bristol . . . to take over his work. To preach to the miners . . . in the open air."

5

THE BRICKFIELDS OF BRISTOL

"*HE'S* ridden a long way!" The stall-owner looked at the man guiding his horse through the narrow street. It stumbled on the slimy cobblestones, and the rider almost slipped from the saddle.

"And ridden hard, too, judging by the horse," answered the woman standing by him, turning back to the tawdry articles displayed on the rough board. "Ah, well, parsons should be used to riding. They go fox-hunting often enough."

"Just about the only thing most of them put their mind to, except eating and drinking with their rich neighbours." He took the small coin the woman handed him for the vegetables she had picked up. "Now if they was all like that parson Whitefield we've been hearing so much about, and thought a bit more about helping country folk like you and me, I might be more interested. I might even go to church sometimes!"

"Ah, you *might*!" laughed the woman. "But I don't think so!"

John Wesley rode on through the crowded lanes of Bristol, past the old Dutch House and down the twisting length of Wine Street. He had set out from London on Thursday; now it was Saturday afternoon. A few minutes later he drew rein outside a little grocer's shop, not far from the pillory and the whipping-post. This was George Whitefield's lodging.

It had been a stiff ride, but he had hardly noticed the country he passed through. He had not really wanted to come at all, and yet he could not stay in London. Charles had angrily denounced their friend George Whitefield's open air preaching as silly and wrong; to the end of his life he was to be critical of anything that was not customary in the Church of England, though he came to see that many things his brother did were necessary, and joined in his adventures with him. Some of John's friends urged him to go, others pressed him to refuse Whitefield's request. At last John had put two pieces of paper in a bowl. One said "Go"; the other said "Stay". John had put his hand in and drawn one. It was the slip which said "Go". Throughout the long ride, he had wondered if he had done right. Even now that he had reached Bristol, he had only made up his mind to see what was happening.

He hung his horse's reins over a post outside the shop and went in.

*   *   *

Late into the night he and Whitefield talked and prayed. John insisted that he had come, not to take over George's work, but simply to judge

46

for himself if it were right. The next morning they were up at dawn and John set out with an uneasy mind, to share in one of the busiest Sundays he had ever known.

April sunshine broke through the clouds as he followed Whitefield to the bowling green in the Pithay, where crowds of people had already gathered. John stood near his friend and watched the faces of the people as they listened. It struck him that they were the same kind of people he had seen through the window of their rooms in London; people he had wanted to talk to, to preach to; ordinary, poor, working people who were never found in church. Could it be, after all, that God was showing him the way?

From the bowling green they set out for Hanham Mount, at Kingswood. Once it had been a lovely, royal park; now, this wide area outside the city of Bristol was covered with slag-heaps, huge piles of earth and rubbish. It was dirty and depressing and what was worse were the rows and rows of "houses" John saw wherever he looked. He supposed they were houses. Certainly men and women lived in them. But, so far as he could see, they were no more than square brick boxes, dirty outside and probably filthy inside, judging by most of the children, who were thin and half-naked. Yet, as soon as they saw Whitefield, hundreds of these people surged towards him. Their sullen faces broke into smiles, and the children fought each other to get near him and hold his hand. There was an even bigger crowd of people not far away at Rose Green, where George Whitefield preached for the third time that day. At each place, he told them the same thing. He would have to leave Bristol. God had called him to preach again in America. When they asked what was to happen while he was away, he made the same reply at each place.

"God, who sends me away, will send someone to take my place!"

Each time he said it, John avoided his glance. He could not pretend to be deaf to his friend's words, however, as they walked back to the city, where the river gleamed silver in the early spring sunlight. He was near the river, running through the centre of the city where sailing ships rode at anchor, that same evening. He had agreed to go and talk to a little company of people who gathered in Nicholas Street. George Whitefield was not far away, at a similar meeting at a house in Baldwin Street. There were few to listen to John, but the house where Whitefield was preaching was so filled with people that he could not even get upstairs and into the room. Instead, he had to climb to the roof of the house next door, scramble across the slippery tiles, and drop through a window into the room where his friends were waiting. This extraordinary beginning to the meeting, however, was not so important as its end.

George Whitefield looked round the room when the meeting was over. "My good friend the

48

Reverend John Wesley came from London yesterday. He has been with me to Kingswood to-day. He will preach in the brickyard at the end of St. Philip's Fields to-morrow morning."

Back in their rooms, he told John what he had promised and, before dawn, he was riding to Gloucester on the way to London. At first John was angry, for he had not agreed to help, but in the end he decided to preach in the morning as Whitefield had done—just once. He thought of how greatly he had wanted to avoid going to the meeting in Aldersgate Street, and how God had spoken to him there. Perhaps, little as he wanted to do it, God was going to use this occasion in the same way. He set out for the brickyard.

To his astonishment, there were more people than there had been in the Pithay to listen to Whitefield the day before. He looked round at their eager, curious faces. There were no hymns, no prayers. He could only speak to them, as he had seen George do. He climbed on to a little mound and said a quiet prayer. There was a deep silence.

"I have come to you in the name of Jesus. He, too, spoke to the people in the fields. At the very beginning He told them why He had come. 'The Spirit of the Lord God is upon me, because He hath anointed me to preach the Gospel to the poor ...'" The three thousand people listened to the clear, well-pitched voice. Many broke into tears as he spoke of God's love for them. Others

49

came and stood on the outskirts of the crowd, or sat on the clay-banks.

"Mr. Whitefield was right," more than one man said to his neighbours when it was over, in their deep West-country voices. "God has taken him away—and sent a greater man in his place!"

By the time it was over, John, himself too, knew that what he had done was right. The closed pulpits of London and Bristol were going to be used to send the message of Jesus into the fields and villages and town-squares of England. What he had begun in the brickfields, John knew in his heart he would never be able to stop.

*   *   *

Within a few days he had spoken at half a dozen places in Bristol, and ridden out to Bath, the fashionable centre of England outside London. Everywhere the results were the same. People asked him to talk to them, to tell them how they could be forgiven for their sins, and went away happier than they had been in their lives. Very soon he came to see that this was producing another problem. The clergymen of Bath and Bristol did not like him. He hardly worried about that. But they had no time, either, for the people he brought to God. They would not give them the Sacrament in their churches and, even when they went to church, the rest of the congregation made it very plain that they were not wanted. They were poor, ill-clothed and for the most part unable to read and write. Another thing John saw very clearly was that, if they were going to keep the new faith they had found, they would have to meet together to learn and talk more about it. What could he do?

He remembered the "societies" he had helped to gather together in London, and the "bands" at Herrnhut, in Germany. These were the very things for them. Somehow, all the things he had seen and done in the last year or so seemed to be fitting in with each other. He gathered those who had been converted into little groups, met with them night after night, and found other good men and women who were also able to lead them and would look after them when he left.

One day, in one of the "bands", a thoughtful man took him aside. "You're too successful in your preaching, brother Wesley! We can't get all the people who come into these little rooms. What are we going to do?"

John had been thinking the same thing himself for some time. He had his answer ready. "We must build a place for them to meet in." The others looked surprised at the suggestion. "And, what is more," John went on, "I think I know the very place. I have seen a piece of land between Broadmead and the Horsefair where we could put just the kind of building we need. Indeed, I've already had a word with the owners, and I think they are willing to sell it to me."

"But what will the clergymen say when they

find you're building a meeting-place? What will the Bishop of Bristol say?"

John smiled grimly. "I've already seen the Bishop, my friend. He tried to stop me preaching here in Bristol. I told him the world was my parish and I would preach wherever I wished."

"But can't he stop you?"

"No one can stop me preaching. Just as no one can stop us building a meeting-place for people who aren't welcome in the parish churches." He turned away. "Come and see this land I've found in the Horsefair."

John was right. No one tried to prevent the building going up after all. It was a simple place that he had planned, with a big room for worship and smaller rooms for the "band-meetings". A month or two after he had first arrived in Bristol, John stood amongst the stones and wood, with the walls partly finished and the open sky above, for the roof had not been begun. The "Methodists" of Bristol crowded round him, sitting where they could, or standing outside the building. In the shell of the first Methodist church ever to be built John preached and dedicated the building. Very soon afterwards he was riding back to London, to tell his friends what had been happening and to see what God had for him to do there.

6

ENGLAND CATCHES FIRE

MOORFIELDS, the open space in the middle
of the City of London, was crowded, even
though it was only seven o'clock on a Sunday
morning. Every minute more and more people
came hurrying along the alleys and the cobbled
streets. Merchants in their sober clothes, apprentices who would later be wrestling on the common, and children who would be playing hide-
and-seek amongst the bushes, were all quieter
than usual as they followed the crowds.

A passer-by caught the sleeve of a hurrying
apprentice. "Here, you," he said, "what's going
on to-day in Moorfields? There can't be a public
hanging—not in Moorfields, and on a Sunday,
surely?"

"It's that man John Wesley—the parson who
was turned out of all the churches. He's going to
preach here this morning."

The idler looked astonished. "Preach? Where?
Not in the open air, surely? I never heard of
such a thing in my life."

"Yes," said the apprentice, tugging his sleeve
loose. "They say he's been doing it in Bristol for
months in the fields. Even got the better of Beau
Nash, the King of Bath, he did."

"I think I'll come with you. There might be some sport. A queer kind of parson he must be to go on like this. Probably a bit mad."

Over the heads of the crowd they saw a slim figure mounting a wooden platform. The apprentice pointed. "Look, there he is. He's beginning to speak already. We'd better push a bit nearer. We'll never hear him at this distance." Then, in the silence, a clear voice reached them. It seemed as if he could be heard all over Moorfields.

John Wesley had no tricks of oratory. He did not pretend to be an actor, nor did he amuse the crowd or frighten them. He never shouted or waved his fist. He just spoke, and his words reached everyone who listened. He spoke simply about God, His hatred of wrong-doing and His love for all men, rich and poor. When he had finished he prayed, as he had preached, without a book, and got down from the platform. There were many who pressed forward to ask him where they might talk to him quietly, and others who said that his words had changed their lives.

*   *   *

Later the same afternoon, John set out to walk across London to the little village of Newington and, through it, to the common at Kennington. Here, too, there were crowds—of a very different kind. There were no important business men or careful apprentices. Instead, there were evil-looking men, drunken women, pickpockets, thieves and vagabonds with no homes who slept on the commons or under the hedges, or haunted the town streets in order to rob lonely wanderers. On a Sunday afternoon there were some fifteen thousand rough folk at Kennington—and, on a Monday morning, there would be more still to see half a dozen men hanged in public from a rough gallows. John looked a strange figure, with his neat hair, clean face and tidy, black suit as he walked through the crowds.

"Are you come to preach to us, parson?" a woman shouted.

"Hey, boys," yelled a dirty youth, "come and see what's here. This'll be better than a cock-fight." He picked up a handful of earth as he spoke, ready to fling it at the preacher.

"Give him something to stand on! Mind yourself, you in front! He's so short we can't see him!"

John clambered on a barrow and held up a hand for silence. "My name is John Wesley," he began. "What I have to say to you is important because it is God's own word. 'Look unto me, and be ye saved, all the ends of the earth.' Those words are God's message to you all." He did not condemn them for what they were, as some preachers did. He spoke again of God's love, of what their lives could be if they turned to God from their evil ways. The boy with the lump of dirt hardly felt it slip out of his hand to the ground. Evil faces softened and tears stood in their eyes as he spoke.

"When can you come and talk to us again?" There were dozens who asked the same question. John looked at them and thought what an astonishing thing it was that God should be using him, a scholar and an Oxford don, to take His word to such people.

"As soon as I can," he answered. "But tomorrow, for a little while, I must ride back to Bristol."

His real life-work had begun in earnest in London and Bristol and, riding between the two for the rest of the summer, he had the first proper taste of the travelling existence that was to be his for the remainder of his days.

*   *   *

It was a cold, icy winter that year and it started early with heavy frosts. John knew that he could not expect people to gather in the bitter weather. The Sunday holiday-makers of Moorfields stayed indoors, more often than not, and John's eager listeners grew almost blue with cold. It was after he had finished speaking one morning that a stranger came up to him.

"You must forgive me for interfering like this. I am not one of your Methodists, but I am interested in what you're doing."

John held out his hand. "All men who love God are my friends. Methodists, you know, are the friends of all and the enemies of none."

"I well believe it. Now, sir. I have just walked

down the lane from the Lord Mayor's kennels, where he keeps his hunting-hounds. Just across there." He pointed to the far corner of Upper Moorfields. "By the side of that lane is the old Foundery. You won't remember—you were too young then—but it was blown up in an explosion years ago when they were melting down the guns we'd captured from the French."

"Yes?" John looked puzzled.

"It has never been used since. I understand you could buy it for a hundred and fifty pounds. A few hundreds more would turn it into the very kind of building you really need. You would have somewhere for your Methodists to meet, in sunshine or snow."

"Sir"—John's voice shook a little with emotion —"I believe God has sent you to me. You're right. It is the very place I could use. Now I think of it, there are other buildings in ruins, too."

The stranger nodded. "The church which belonged to the French refugees, you mean? Yes, indeed. There's one in Spital Fields, and one in Seven Dials. There's another in Southwark, as well, over the river. You should look at them." He turned on his heel, his long coloured coat clutched round his body against the cold. "I bid you good day, sir." Almost before the stranger could lift his big three-cornered, gold-laced hat from his wig, John was speeding across the grass of Upper Moorfields towards the ruined Foundery.

Before long, it was turned into a church. A bell, hung in the small belfry which John had erected, called the people to worship every morning at five o'clock. There were plain benches below, and galleries above them, where men and women sat separately, as they always did in the early preaching-places. Part of the building was turned into a band-room, where Methodists met to talk together about their faith and their problems. During the day, a school was held there. Above it, rooms were built for John's own use when he was in London, and there his mother Susannah, now moved from Emily's school in Gainsborough to London, lived and talked with John's friends. In Mrs. Wesley's room, something happened which was to affect the future of Methodism.

*   *   *

John had been in Bristol. Business and the weather delayed his return. As he rode along the London road from Bath he wondered what had happened to the service he was supposed to have taken. They would have had no preacher. Charles was not there, and, as John always insisted, only ordained ministers had the right to preach. Other people might help in the little meetings—Thomas Maxfield, for instance, a young man who had been converted in Bristol, had been told by John that he might do this. But they must not preach. That was the clergyman's work, and no one else's. Well, John supposed, they would have sung Charles's hymns, and prayed, and read the Bible and gone home.

At the Foundery he had a shock, and when he walked into his mother's room upstairs, he looked furiously angry. He nodded to his mother and pulled off his riding-coat.

"My dear son," said Susannah, surprised, "whatever is the matter? Has somebody threatened to have you put in prison for preaching in the open air? You look very bitter about something."

"I *am* angry, Mother." His voice was harsh. "I understand young Maxfield has been doing my work for me!" There was a sarcastic tone in the words. "He has been preaching, has he not? In the service? I never asked him to do this, and I shall dismiss him from the Methodist Society."

"John . . ."

He would not listen. "Charles and I have been well trained. Our English clergymen have studied the Bible and been prepared for their work. Thomas can know little or nothing. If we let men like him preach they will be a danger and a hindrance, not a help. He may say almost anything. And, the trouble is, because he calls himself a Methodist, people will listen."

Mrs. Wesley held up her hand, and John fell silent. "Listen to me. I heard Thomas Maxfield preach. He spoke clearly and well. He has a *call*, from God, to preach—just as much as you have, even though he has never had a chance, like you, of going to a university. How many Methodists are there?" she asked, more sharply.

"More than I can deal with, here and in Bristol."

"And there will be more still, before long. And you will be less able to deal with them. You are not the only man in England who can preach, John. Even with Charles by your side you will never be able to catch up with your Methodist flame. It will spread ahead of you, and on every side. You must have helpers—preachers who can be trusted to say what you yourself would say."

John stood very still. It was as though he was looking far beyond the little room in the Foundery, to the wide commons and fields of the English countryside, to the smoky industrial cities of the Midlands and the north, to the busy tin-mines of Cornwall. Everywhere people were waiting for the message he had spoken in Bristol and London. They *must* have a chance to hear it. In his vision, for a moment, he saw men and women all over the country, gathered into little "societies" like those he had already set up. He saw villages becoming tidier, towns cleaner, men more hard-working, women happier, little children going to school, homeless boys and girls being taken into orphanages. Methodism was less than two years old, but John was already beginning to see what it might do. Was it too much to say that God was going to use this new spiritual movement to change England in the years ahead? If that was so, it would need more than himself and his brother, and perhaps a few friendly clergymen in wide parishes, to do it. He must have helpers.

"I must have helpers. Yes; I think you are right, Mother. And you say Thomas Maxfield is fitted for the work?"

His mother nodded. She was a very old lady now, and she sounded tired. "Yes, John. I am sure of it." As clearly as John she saw what was likely to happen through this wonderful movement that John had begun. She pointed to the door. "Go and tell him so, John."

Thomas Maxfield was the first "lay preacher" in Methodism—but very soon there were others who joined him at John's request. John's dream began to come true. The Methodist message of hope and love was beginning to be heard all over the country. John and Charles were familiar figures as they rode into the north, to Epworth and Newcastle, and into the west, to Bristol and, far beyond it, to Wales or Cornwall.

But, as Methodism spread, the tide began to turn, and angry voices were raised against the Wesleys and their people.

7

RIOTS EVERYWHERE

"WHAT do you reckon's going on in there? Eh?" A group of men, walking home from the alehouse in the village, stood still, while their leader pointed to a cottage across the fields.

"Ah, that's what *I* should like to know." The voice was thick and slurred from heavy drinking. "Methodists, they are. Rotten, spyin' Methodists!"

"Spies—that's it!" The third man caught his friend by the edge of his ragged coat. "Everyone knows there's plots goin' on all the time to get rid of King George. Why, Prince Charlie's sitting there in France, only just across the Channel, waiting to come over and kill the king and put us all in prison."

"But what have *they* got to do with it? Eh?" The first speaker pointed again at the cottage window.

"Don't be so daft, Jack," the third man answered. "Everyone knows this Wesley feller is a Roman Catholic in disguise. He's one of Prince Charlie's best spies."

"You mean these Methodists are in the pay of the French?"

"Course they are! Everybody knows that; except you, so it seems. Let's teach them a lesson!" He led the drunken group towards the cottage, stumbling over the mole-hills and rabbit-holes in the field.

Inside the cottage, half a dozen people were gathered round a table, reading by the dim light of a candle. Suddenly a stone crashed through the window, knocking the candle over as it rebounded from a woman's shoulder. Outside, noisy shouts and laughter broke out. Two or three more stones hurtled into the room. By the time the tiny Methodist society had opened the door and re-lit the candle the voices were growing fainter as the ignorant drunkards shambled back across the fields to the track through the village. By the light of the candle, the Methodists turned again to the Bible on the table, finished their reading and knelt to pray.

*   *   *

The trouble was that, though many people had heard of the Methodists, very few people really knew much about them. Not a few people honestly but foolishly believed they were spies on the side of the Young Pretender who invaded England in 1745. Magistrates treated them as disturbers of the peace, because of their crowded open air meetings. Lazy, careless clergymen helped to turn the mobs on them because the Methodist preachers had harsh things to say of parsons who preferred drinking and hunting to their proper work of preaching and caring for their parishes. Honest ministers, disliking the strange new ways of services in the fields, lay preachers and week-night cottage meetings, opposed Wesley and his helpers because they believed the old traditions of the Church of England were better and wiser. Everywhere the common people were desperately poor, ignorant and rough. They worked hard from dawn until darkness, when they fell wearily asleep in the dirty hovels in which they lived, or drank themselves senseless in the alehouses. Their only recreations were the occasional fairs, and the more frequent bull-baitings and cock-fights. Knowing nothing of any real reason for mobbing the Methodist preachers as they stood up to speak, they were still only too glad to bait a man instead of a bull, and joined with coarse enjoyment in flinging him into the pond or setting the dogs on him. John and Charles Wesley themselves were often violently attacked by the mobs.

Near the Whitechapel Road, on Coverlet Fields, in London, John talked to an eager crowd. At the edge of it he noticed some ruffians whispering and laughing. They went off for a while, but were soon back—driving a herd of cows ahead of them. They urged them towards the crowd but John saw, thankfully, that the animals dodged back and raced into the fields again. Then, he saw the men bend down and pick something up. A shower of stones flew through the air. His voice never faltered but, suddenly, he staggered. A stone had hit him between the eyes. With calm courage, he wiped the blood away with his handkerchief and went on talking as though nothing had happened, while the attackers slunk away across the fields.

At Pensford, in the Midlands, he had a closer view of the mob—and the bull. This time he had no crowd to begin with. He simply borrowed a table from the inn, put it in the middle of the village green, climbed on it and began to preach. Hardly had he started when a mob, which knew he was coming and had been paid by the local parson and the magistrates to get rid of him, burst on to the green. Ahead of them they drove a maddened, frightened bull, thrusting it towards the preacher. Every time it swerved to right or left and only once did it blunder towards him. Then John bent down, turned its head neatly as it came, so that it swung past the table, the mangy dogs snapping at its heels, and went on speaking as though nothing had happened. Furious at being cheated, the mob flung themselves against the table. As it fell, they smashed it to pieces, trying to grab John's coat as he tumbled off. He did not fall far. When his tormentors had gathered their wits together, they noticed that he had been snatched from the table by his friends as it crashed over and was now being carried away safely on their shoulders.

*   *   *

More than once, John was nearly killed by the

5

rioters. It was like that in Falmouth, when he had gone to visit a Methodist who was ill. Hardly had he arrived when a mob began to beat on the door of the house.

"Go out through the back," he ordered the sick woman and her daughter. When they protested that it was he who should escape, he pushed them towards the door. "Someone must stay and protect the house. If they find you here and me gone they will probably pull it down over your heads."

No sooner had they gone than there was a tremendous crash at the front of the house. The street door had been broken in and feet were heard on the stairs.

"What shall we do now, sir?" John turned, astonished, to find a little Cornish serving-maid still in the room.

He smiled, confidently, "We must pray, child," he said.

"But hadn't you better run away?" she asked tearfully.

John listened to the din in the passage. "Through that rabble, out there?" He smiled. "It would be a bit difficult to run through *them*, I think. No, pray that God will quieten them." She noticed that John's praying was very private, and he did not need to go on his knees to do it. He was busy taking down a large looking-glass as he spoke to save it from being broken. Across the cobbled stones from the harbour half a dozen

66

sailors came running from a privateer riding at anchor. They had no idea what was happening, but it promised to be exciting.

"What's the matter? Who's in there? A murderer? Break the door down!" The sailors' voices rose high above the din. With a rending noise the door gave way and John faced the crowd in the passage.

"What do you want?" he asked. "Have I done anything to harm you? Or you?" He pointed to a man in the crowd, who shook his head. "Or you?" He stepped forward and the men backed away in front of him. Out in the street he faced the rest of the mob. "Are you going to let me speak to you?" he asked.

"Let him speak!" the sailors shouted from the door, won over by the courage of the quiet, calm little man. "Let's hear what he has to say!" There was no stool to stand on, so he spoke from where he was, hemmed in by the crowd. There was a movement here and there, and John noticed three or four stylishly dressed gentlemen, probably magistrates, and a clergyman, closing in on him. It looked as if he were going to be arrested, but he went on preaching. The people were so still that his voice reached the edge of the crowd. He prayed, and was finished.

"Where do you wish to go, sir?" asked one of the gentlemen to John's great surprise. "No one will touch you while we are here." With the mob at their heels, now silenced for the time being, they walked to the house where John was intending to stay.

He would have liked to have mounted his horse and ridden away, but his friends were still afraid of the crowd. Instead, they took him through the house, down the back garden to the river's edge. The tide was full, as the sea swept up through Falmouth Bay. He dropped into a little boat. Some of his friends slipped back to collect his horse, whilst the rest rowed him towards Penryn. They moved in as much silence as they could, but the oars slapped against the rising tide and, before long, the mob saw how they had been cheated. It was dark now, and the moon was a bright crescent in the sky. There was light enough, however, to see that the mob had raced across the fields and up the riverside to be at Penryn before him. They were massed on the steps by the wharf, ready to fling him into the water as he got out of the boat.

A moment's hesitation might still have cost him his life. He stepped calmly from the rocking boat and mounted the slippery steps. The crowd parted as he did so. He walked through them as if he did not notice them until he reached the top of the steps. The ringleader stood there, his hands on his hips, his rough hair blowing in the wind. He glared as John came towards him. Just behind him was John's horse. John looked at him for a moment.

"Good night, my friend," he said quietly. A

moment later he had sprung into the saddle. Still motionless, the ruffian watched him, too startled to believe what he saw. Only when they heard the hoof-beats of the horse trotting up the road towards Truro and Redruth did the mob realize that their victim had escaped, after all.

Such courage as that, coming from John's deep faith that he was God's messenger to England, soon began to make an impression on the mobs, just as his preaching moved almost everyone who heard it. His writings, too, were becoming known to thousands who had never seen him. In town and village, in cottage and noble mansion, his name was spoken with a new respect. Methodism passed through its age of persecution. The tide had turned again.

8

THE KNIGHT RIDES ON

"JOHN WESLEY is dying!"

The news spread round England like wild-fire. He had tuberculosis, and had collapsed in Bristol. Methodism was to lose one of its leaders, though his brother Charles was still very much alive, preaching, riding and writing hymns. It was impossible to think what would happen to Methodism without John's steadying hand.

"But it's not surprising," people said to one another. "Think of all that riding, in all kinds of weather. Standing preaching, soaked to the skin. No one could put up with it for long!"

Fortunately, it was not quite true. He *had* collapsed, and at one point John himself thought he was nearly at the end of his life. He retired to the Hot Wells, near the Avon River, at the beginning of the gorge that runs for some miles towards the river-mouth. Weary and in pain, he tossed about in a fever, getting up from bed whenever he could to write careful notes about the New Testament for his followers to read, and answering the letters that reached him. Had he had an easy life, coddling himself from wind and cold, he might very well have died. Because, from the early years at Charterhouse, when he had run his daily mile round the Green, he had disciplined his body to stand up to almost any strain, he began to get better. Before long, he was on the road once more.

Eighteenth-century roads were very different from our own. Between Kensington and West-minster—to-day, both part of London—it was sometimes impossible to travel at all because of the deep sea of mud. Along many of the main roads the carriages made ruts two feet or more deep. Huge stones blocked the roads, and bliz-zards covered the tracks across the moors and commons which John often followed. It would have taken more than storms or highwaymen to keep John off the roads. The saddle was more of a home to him than his house at the Foundery, his rooms at Kingswood or the New Room in Bristol. Day after day he set off early in the morn-ing, as soon as it was light, stopped after a few miles to preach on a village green, rode on again until mid-morning to do the same. Probably he would preach again in the afternoon and once more before it was dark. During the day he would often ride something like thirty or forty miles, and he would end by stabling his horse, before he attended to his own needs, and then, after supper, talking to a little "society" of Methodists by lamp-light or candlelight in the room where they met each week.

*   *   *

He was riding along a lonely road one afternoon when he heard a rustling in the hedge. He thought nothing of it. Even had he noticed he would have put it down to a fox or a badger. As he rode, he left the horse's reins loose, allowing it to choose its own way over the stony track. He himself had his eyes on a book, resting on the front of his saddle. He never wasted time. He read wherever he went, as people to-day read in a bus or a train. Now, however, the rustling grew louder, and his horse jerked its head in fright.

John looked up, and slipped the book into his pocket. A moment later, the bushes parted. A tall chestnut mare was edged out into the road, with a man in long brown riding-coat and three-cornered hat on her back. John could hardly see his face, for his eyes and nose were covered by a black silk mask. It did not need the pistol in the man's hand to tell him that here was a highwayman.

"Your money, parson!" The pistol was lifted. "And no tricks, mind! You can't get away!"

John thought for a moment. This enemy, unlike those in the riotous crowds, was not to be stared out and scared away by a show of courage.

"Quick, now. There's no hope of anyone else coming. I made sure of that from the top of the hill." He moved his horse forward a pace or two. "Your purse. Throw it to me."

From his pocket John drew an old purse. It looked light as he tossed it to the highwayman, and the robber laughed as he looked inside. "That's small enough, in all conscience. Where do you keep the rest, eh?"

"It is all I have. My name is John Wesley—and if you have ever heard it you will know that I have no time to get or spend much money."

"Wesley, eh? So I've stopped the man all England listens to. Well, don't think that that's going to get your purse back again. I can spend it—if you can't!" He turned his horse.

"One day"—John's voice rang clear over the downs—"the time may come when you regret your way of life. Remember, then; Jesus Christ forgives sins!"

There was no answer but a crack of the riding crop as the highwayman cantered swiftly off to seek a wealthier victim.

*   *   *

It was about this time that he faced another danger—that of drowning. He was on his way to Grimsby, but when he reached the Trent he found the river in flood. The boatmen stared at him when he asked whether they were not going to ferry him across.

"We're not so mad as to try it in weather like this!" they replied.

"But," John urged, "I have to preach in Grimsby. The congregation will be expecting me."

The surly boatmen sneered. "Let them wait.

73

What good can sermons do, anyway? If you think we're going to risk our necks to get a parson over this flood just because he wants to go and preach in Grimsby, you're mistaken!"

It was the boatmen who were mistaken. John's pleading, and that of some other would-be passengers, made the boatmen give way in the end. With six men, two women and three horses in it, the ferry boat set out. The men strained at the oars. The flood tide swung the boat round, and round again. The women screamed, but only John tried to attend to them, and he found he could not move. From side to side the boat rocked, shipping water at every lurch against the tide. The three horses leapt from the boat in terror, John's amongst them, and swam to shore in their own way, landing far down the river bank. At last, with a final swing that seemed certain to capsize the boat, they reached the further bank. The women were heaved out, and five men stood on the bank.

"Where's the parson?" they asked. "Come on, you. It was you who wanted to come. What's the matter? Have you fainted or something?" They moved to the side of the boat and looked in. John lay on the bottom, an iron crowbar through the lace of his boot pinning him to the side.

"It was as well the boat came to the shore safely, by the mercy of God, or I should have certainly gone to the bottom with it," John said calmly, as he finally climbed out. "But the congregation in

Grimsby will not be disappointed of their service after all, my friends." He tramped down the bank, calling to his frightened, wet horse.

*   *   *

There were other things besides weather, high-waymen and flooded rivers which made travelling hard for the gallant little preacher. One of them was that he had no real home of his own. In Bristol he had his rooms and a library, as he had at the Foundery in London and in Newcastle. Everywhere else in England he had to depend on the kindness of his friends. This was easy where he had been before, or was well known. Some-times, however, when he was riding into strange country, the welcome was poor indeed. Cornwall, in the beginning, gave him no welcome at all.

Along the Cornish roads John picked his way as carefully as he could, with a Yorkshire preacher, John Nelson, riding behind him. They were said to be the worst roads in England. Indeed, in the north and west of the county there were no roads at all, and hardly any guide posts across the moors to tell them where they were going.

"It's three days since we slept in a proper bed, sir," said Nelson, as they paused to look over the landscape. They were tired and hungry, and the horses' heads were drooping with weariness.

"*This* doesn't look very hopeful, brother Nelson." John pointed ahead of them. In the distance, on the right, they could see the ocean,

75

reaching to the horizon. Before them stretched desolate moorland. "Can you see a house?"

Nelson put his hand to his eyes. "Not even a trail of smoke anywhere in sight." He pointed to the sun, almost touching the sea. "And it's going to be dark, soon. We shall never find our way in the darkness."

"No hope of getting to an inn to-night, then, brother Nelson."

"They're not worth staying at when we do, sir. They never keep food in for travellers. I suppose most people are wiser than we are, and never travel to Cornwall. What are we going to do?"

John got down from his horse. "The first thing we're going to do, brother, is to eat." He moved across to some bushes a few yards from the track.

"Eat?" Nelson looked astonished as he alighted from his own animal. "What are we going to eat, sir?"

John was already poking amongst the brambles. "Blackberries. That's all there is to eat in Cornwall, so we'll have to do the best we can. There's enough for both of us here. Big ones, too, with plenty of juice to quench your thirst."

"Blackberries!" Nelson's voice was weary. "A nice welcome this is for men who come to preach about God's goodness."

"Times will change, brother Nelson. We shall be welcome in Cornwall before long. See how eagerly the people listen when we talk to them.

76

The tin-miners may be rough and the villagers on the coast may be mostly smugglers now—but they will change in time, and then we shall indeed be welcome. Meanwhile we shall have to sleep, as we did last night, in the first moorland shepherd's hut we can find."

Nelson moved awkwardly from one bush to another. "My skin is almost rubbed off one side already through sleeping on the ground."

"Never mind, you've still got one good side left—and so have I." John popped two or three more berries into his mouth. "But I must admit that this is the best country I ever yet came across for getting an appetite and the worst for getting any food."

John was right. Times did change, not only in Cornwall, but everywhere. Soon he was welcome wherever he went, whether it was in inns, cottages or the great houses of the countryside. Travelling was never easy, though the roads were getting better towards the end of his life. Highwaymen were being driven out of business, and John was never stopped again for his purse.

One day, however, he did meet a man who startled him. He looked like a very respectable citizen, and wore neither mask nor pistols.

"You don't recognize me, sir?" asked the stranger.

"No, I think not—though I've a good memory for faces. Have I met you before?"

"Indeed you have, though you didn't properly

see my face. I owe you some money, sir. I used to be a highwayman, and I once stopped you and robbed you of your purse."

"I shouldn't have recognized you, my friend."

"But *I* know *you*—and I know what you did for me. I want you to know that what you said came true. I changed my ways because, thanks to you, God changed me."

The King's horseman rode on that day with a thankful heart.

9

THE CARRIAGE

JOHN climbed down slowly from his horse. He used to be able to leap down, but now he was an old man and he had to go more carefully. As he walked from his horse towards the big house he limped slightly, but he still walked quickly. His coat was carefully brushed, though his riding breeches were spattered with mud after riding from London. Pausing on the threshold, he took off his three-cornered black hat, and his hair shone silvery in the sunlight.

"Miss Levens is expecting me to call," he told the footman who opened the door. Then, looking at the carriage which stood by the steps, he went on, "It looks as if she has some visitors already."

"No, Mr. Wesley," replied the footman. "Miss Levens is alone."

In the big drawing-room, Miss Levens rose to meet him. Like all Methodists, however rich they might be, she was dressed plainly, in a long dress which swept the ground. "It is good of you to come, Mr. Wesley," she said, holding her hand out for him to touch.

He bowed slightly as he took it. "You asked me to see you about a matter of some importance," he said. "I have been wondering what it might be."

Miss Levens smiled. "I have a present for you, sir."

"A *present*?" John sounded startled. "This is very unusual. I want nothing—though I have very little of my own. My books, of course, and my horse." He laughed lightly. "And of course I have two silver spoons—the only silver or gold I possess!" He looked round, as though searching for the gift.

"I'm afraid it is rather too large to give you in here. Come to the window, sir." She moved across the room, and John joined her. "There, sir. I hope you will enjoy it—and," she added, firmly, "I hope you will *use* it!"

John's face was puzzled as he looked towards the steps, from which a servant was leading his horse away to be groomed and fed. "I see nothing —nothing but the carriage."

"*That*," said Miss Levens, "is your present." She held up her hand as John started to protest. "It is no use to argue. Why, you limp even now as you walk! You have been riding a horse all over England for . . . how many years?"

"Well over thirty, at any rate," John answered.

"It's no use asking how many falls you've had, I suppose? But this last fall has hurt you more than most of the others. You can't go on riding like this in all kinds of weather. In future, sir, I hope you will use the carriage, and save yourself from dying of a chill. Methodism needs you as long as you can live to care for it."

*　　*　　*

At first, John hated the carriage. It seemed like giving in, not to ride horseback. Then, after a while, he found there would be advantages in using it after all, and it soon became almost as familiar on the roads of England as his horse had been. Not so long after he had had it altered as he wished, he drove up to Newcastle. He remembered his first visit very clearly. It was soon after he had begun his work in Bristol and London, and he had only been able to spend a few days there before he handed the preaching over to his brother Charles. Then, he had thought it the worst city in England for drunkenness and swearing. Now, things were very different.

The carriage drew up outside a solid-looking building. As John alighted he heard the subdued murmur of children's voices coming from an open window. A man opened the door and came forward to meet him, his face beaming with delight.

"We're so glad to see you again, Mr. Wesley," he said. "And in your new carriage, too."

"And you're surprised that I allow myself to use it, I expect, after I've spent so long riding horseback?" He drew his friend towards the open door. "It's a great blessing, brother. I would have been wet through again and again riding up from London. In this, I'm as dry as a bone! But, step

81

6

in. See why I like it. You'll have to come out through the same door, I'm afraid!" Looking round, the Newcastle man saw that the far door had been blocked up with a set of bookcases, filled with books. Instead of two seats, the carriage had only one. The other had been built over with a desk that folded out when John wished to write as he travelled.

"I can write as I ride now, sir, while on horseback I could only read. I've written a dozen letters since I got into the carriage this morning, and corrected the proofs of one of my new books, as well as reading." John helped him out as he came down the high steps. "And now, let me look at the children." He followed him into the house and along a passage into a room at the end. It was the room from which the voices had come as he had got out of his carriage. As the door opened, there was silence, and a score of children rose quickly to their feet. All were girls, dressed alike, in very plain clothes. They curtsied as John entered the room.

"Good evening, Mr. Wesley, sir," they said, almost in chorus, their faces full of smiles.

"Good evening," John answered, looking round. He beckoned to a little girl, terribly thin, with her face marked by smallpox, who stood in the front. "Come here, my child. I don't think I know you. What is your name?" he asked as she stepped forward.

"Grace, sir."

"A good name," said John.

"They gave it to me here, sir. I don't know what my proper name is. You see, they brought me to work in the mills when I was too small to remember properly. My mother sold me to a mill-owner because she had too many children already. And then, when I was sick, he didn't want me because I couldn't work." She reached out and took hold of John's hands. "Oh, sir! If it weren't for you I don't know what would have happened to me."

"I don't know what would have happened to any of them if it hadn't been for you, beginning this orphanage, Mr. Wesley," added the man by his side. "It is one of the greatest things you've ever done, starting this place for children who aren't wanted by anybody."

John stood very thoughtfully. "It's a long time ago since I went to Germany to visit the Moravian settlements there," he said. "I told Charles when I came back that I was sure He had sent me for some purpose. Looking back, I see what it was. He wanted me to see the things that I could do in this country when Methodism began to grow. I remember telling Charles that I, too, would like to begin schools for poor children, almshouses for those who were too old to work any longer—and an orphanage for those children who had no one to care for them."

"Well, sir," the orphanage-master answered, "you have them all, now; the almshouses in

London, the school at Kingswood, and this orphanage in Newcastle. It's because you care for people as well as preach to them that folk listen to what you say."

John turned to leave the room. "Yes, brother, we found that out in Oxford, long ago."

*   *   *

John had always liked children, and the Newcastle orphanage and the Kingswood school in Bristol were never out of his mind for long. He planned the school at Bristol with great care, and very often stayed there when he preached in the city. The boys had few holidays, and they rose early and worked hard, but that was true of all the "boarding schools" in England at that time. For them, John wrote English, French, Greek, Hebrew and German grammars, and he made sure that the boys were taught music as well as more "serious" subjects. Most of his time, however, was given to preaching, and to caring for the Methodist "societies" all over the country. Every day it was the same—up early, preaching, visiting and riding from one town to another.

It was on a Sunday that John's carriage rolled along the road from St. Ives to Hayle at about seven o'clock in the morning. With him was Dr. Thomas Coke, a clergyman who had joined the Methodists a few years before and become John's secretary and helper. It might seem early to set out for his Sunday's services, but John began every day very much earlier than that. He had risen at four o'clock, washed and dressed, and by half-past four was praying quietly in a little room looking over the blue sea. Before the carriage arrived, he had read his Bible, looked over the sermons he was going to preach during the day, and had a little breakfast. His words had come true. Cornwall, where he had once had to eat blackberries and sleep in a moorland hut, was a place where he was always welcome.

As they rode along, he looked out of the window at the countryside. There were tin-mines everywhere, and all the five miles from St. Ives to Hayle, little granite villages with their grey houses were clustered along the roadside. The news of his coming had spread ahead of him and, as they came near to Hayle, he found a great crowd blocking the road by the copper-works. Almost all of them were tin-miners or copper-miners. He recalled the riots that used to greet his coming to Cornwall; now, the people were only gathered to persuade him to preach before he went on to Hayle itself. He could not refuse, and took his first service of the day, out of doors.

The Methodist preaching-house itself was interesting enough to make John take out his notebook when he saw it and jot down a few words about it.

"I've never seen a place like it, Thomas," he said to Dr. Coke. "Look at it. It's completely round, and built out of rubbish!"

"Rubbish?"

"Yes," said John, who seemed to know everything. "The square stones are really what is left after they have taken the tin and copper out of the rock. It's called slag. Our Methodists may not have much money—but they have plenty of ideas." He stepped across the rough roadway to the "preaching-house" and waited for Coke to catch up with him. "But somebody has been spending a lot of money for our sakes, I see."

It was quite true. A member of the congregation had made a pot of tea for them, to refresh them after the journey—and tea was then one of the most expensive luxuries in England. The smugglers and sailors who had once tried to kill him now wished to give him the best they had. In the chapel the Methodists had gathered together for John to give them the Sacrament of Holy Communion, which they could very seldom have in their own preaching-places. He met a few people who were in trouble, and one or two others who had been found smuggling.

"You know what our rules are," John said to them sternly, in the little vestry. "Anyone who smuggles is to be turned out of membership in Methodism. It is the same with those who get drunk, or beat their wives, or stay away from the weekly meetings. You can't pray like a Christian on Sunday, and behave wrongly on Monday. You may have one more chance—and one only.

The preacher here in Hayle will remove your name if you are ever found smuggling again."

*   *   *

He was in Redruth, nearly ten miles away, by midday. He had intended to meet the Methodists in one of the preaching-houses, and so he did. By the time he left the church, however, an hour later, to go and have dinner, he could hardly push his way through the crowds outside. By half-past one, there were more people than he had ever seen before in this town which was the centre of the tin-mining industry. He needed the help of the constable to get into the market square. There was no working on Sunday—the Methodists made sure of that—and it was thronged wherever he looked. Then, as he looked up, he saw to his astonishment that not only were all the windows filled with listeners from the villages round about, but the low pitched roofs of the houses round the market place were covered with people, too. He prayed, and then preached for nearly an hour. They were still in the market an hour later, singing some of his brother Charles's hymns, when he left the town to drive out to Busveal, a few miles away. Here was the famous Gwennap Pit, a deep, wide hole in the midst of the fields, where some old tin-mines had caved in many years previously. John had preached there almost every time since he had first come to Cornwall, and long before he reached it this September Sunday there were

87

twenty thousand people waiting to listen to him again. He could hear the sound of their hymn-singing rolling out across the fields as he came nearer. *O for a thousand tongues to sing*; *Love Divine, all loves excelling*; *Jesu, Lover of my soul*— one after the other his brother's best known hymns rose into the Cornish air, sung, as John always said, as nobody else in England could sing them.

Before the night finished, he had gone back to Redruth, giving the Sacrament to the Methodist people there, and talked from supper-time until bed-time. Since four o'clock in the morning he had driven some twenty-five miles, taken half a dozen services in three different towns and villages, and talked with scores of people. When John spent that particular Sunday he was eighty-four years old. It was not an unusual Sunday. Every day of the week, every week of the year, was very much the same.

10

BOTH SIDES OF THE OCEAN

THOMAS COKE rode into the yard outside the New Room in the Horsefair, in Bristol. Beside the entrance to the chapel was a little stable. He led his horse into it, pulled off its saddle, saw there was water in the trough and corn in the manger before he entered the chapel. He looked up as he went in, towards the windows in the roof. John Wesley's own rooms were built above the chapel and the roof windows opened into them. As Thomas looked up, he saw the old man standing there, his face thin and his hair silvery-white. Thomas waved back, and went quickly upstairs.

"You know that I've sent you to places where I couldn't go myself, Thomas," said John, a little while later, after they had had something to eat.

"All over the country. Yes. And to Ireland and Wales, too." Thomas Coke was a short man, dark-haired, red-faced, and he always seemed to be excited about something. "Do you want me to go somewhere else?" he asked eagerly.

"I do," John answered seriously. "I am going to send you to America."

"America!" Coke nearly jumped from his chair in excitement. "But why?"

"Ever since the American colonies fought their war of independence and broke free from Britain I have been having letters from them. There are hardly any ministers left in the land. Our Methodist people are calling out for help. I want you to go and see how they are getting on. You are to take two of our English preachers with you." John sighed. "I wish I could go myself, Thomas. I would like to see what they've made of America in the fifty years since I was there. But I'm too old for that sort of journey now—three months at sea and another three months coming back. Besides, I have too much to do here. So you must go instead." He pulled a map towards him, putting his finger on place after place. "See, there are Methodists here in New York and Baltimore, on the coast. And up here in the mountains. There, see, that is wild country—forests and prairies— but we have Methodists there, too. I believe we can do a great deal to make America a very fine country."

"As Methodism, under your guidance, has done in England," commented Dr. Coke.

"Yes, Thomas, God has done great things in England—though I wish I could have done more."

"No man could have done more, sir." That was true enough. "You have not only changed men and women, you have changed villages and towns. You have given people, who were ignorant and poverty-stricken, something worth living for. You have begun schools and orphanages and encouraged others to do the same. You have written more books, and published more, than any other man in the country. You have . . ."

John held up his hand. "That's enough, Thomas! You'd better start thinking about America—I want you to leave almost at once."

*　　*　　*

That was not Thomas Coke's only visit to America. He made another a little later, taking another three preachers with him. This began as a disastrous voyage, and after more than three months of storms, when the ship was driven right off its course for America, they were forced into anchorage at the little West Indian island of Antigua, on Christmas Eve. Dr. Coke described to John Wesley how he had been met by a man with a lantern as they walked up from the quay early on Christmas morning.

"He took us home, though he was going to an early morning service, and let us wash and gave us breakfast. Then he asked me to preach at the service he was taking. It was four o'clock in the morning when I entered the church." He paused, remembering the scene. "I have never seen anything like it before, sir. The whole church was crowded with people—and every one, except ourselves, was black. They were all negroes and all slaves."

"So Methodism has begun to travel to the heathen, brother Coke," said John softly.

"Yes, sir. And Mr. Baxter, who met us, and who has carried on the work there and built the chapel for the slaves, says that *that* is your doing, too."

John sat very quietly. "In a way, I suppose it is. The first man to care for the slaves and hold services for them was a planter to whom I preached in a village outside London forty years ago."

Coke broke in. "Yes. But he died and the work would have stopped if you hadn't suggested to Mr. Baxter that he should try his fortune in the West Indies. You knew that he was the kind of man who would carry on the work."

"John Baxter was a good carpenter—and a good preacher. He had a chance to go to the Royal Dockyard in Antigua. I told him to go, yes. But I did not really know what would happen—that *this* would be the result—when I persuaded him." John shook his head, a look of wonder on his face. "I have never had any idea what would happen, Thomas, and yet from the beginning God has been guiding everything I have done." He sat quietly, hardly moving until Coke rose, knowing that John wanted to be alone, and went out, saying that he had better go and look after his horse.

The great man watched him through the window, as he went out of the New Room. He thought of how it looked when he first preached in it, while it was still being built, a month or so after he had first begun preaching in the open air. He thought of that hard ride to Bristol, in answer to George Whitefield's letter, and of how he had hated going, and hated even more the thought of breaking away from church services, of preaching in the fields. He thought of how he went to Aldersgate Street that night in May, with the sunset over the roofs of London, and of how he had not wanted to go there, either.

"I have never known what was going to happen," he said to himself. "And yet, God has always been there, leading and directing me. And," he added quietly, "the best of all is, God is with us still." He stood up, abruptly, breaking his day-dream, and went across to his desk. It was tidy, as it always was. He took up his quill pen, and a clean sheet of writing paper. There was work to do, and, unless he got on, it would be dark and he would have to light the candles before his letters were written.

*　　*　　*

There was always work to do, right to the end of his life. He toured through the Midlands, northern England and right to the north of Scotland a few months before he fell ill for the last time, and preached only a week or so before he died. It was at his charming little house, attached to the new chapel at City Road, in London, that he spent his last days, with his friends coming to see

93

him day by day. The last words he ever said, just before he died, were the ones that had been in his mind over the past few years.

"The best of all is, God is with us!"

To that quiet little house where he lived at the end of his life, not far from all the bustle of London's busy traffic, people from all over the world now make their way. His books, his papers, his letters, the things he used are there for his modern followers to see. It is almost as though he were there himself, quietly watching Indians and Africans, Australians and Americans, men and women of all colours, as they pass in and out. The Church he began still goes on, and the handful of Methodists in Bristol and London has grown into something like fifty million, all over the earth. But John Wesley himself does not belong just to Methodism. We all owe him something for what he did for England and the world. He belongs to the whole Church.